Portrait of AUSTIN

 FARCOUNTRY
PRESS

PHOTOGRAPHY BY **LAURENCE PARENT**

To my wife, Patricia.

*Thanks to Patricia, Michelle, and Jason Parent, Lora Hufton,
Sienna Jones, Robin Harris, Jenny Lambright, Keri Thomas,
David Bamberger, Colleen Gardner, Scott Grote,
and Bob and Janis Daemmrich
for their help with this book.*

Right: Forty miles from Austin, thirty-acre Westcave Preserve protects a limestone canyon dotted with rare plants and cypress trees (seen here), as well as grasslands, wildflower meadows, and a forty-foot waterfall.

Title page: Orange light bathes the top of the University of Texas Tower, signaling a Longhorn sports team victory.

Front cover: The vivid lights of downtown Austin streak the surface of Lady Bird Lake with color.

Back cover: Looking up from the Texas State Capitol's rotunda into its majestic dome.

Front flap: Spring-fed Bull Creek flows through the forty-eight-acre park of the same name. One of Austin's dedicated off-leash dog parks, it includes barbeque pits and picnic areas, basketball and volleyball courts, multipurpose fields, a fishing pier, and a swimming area.

ISBN 10: 1-56037-480-2
ISBN 13: 978-1-56037-480-0

For more information on our books, write Farcountry Press, P.O. Box 5630, Helena, MT 59604; call (800) 821-3874; or visit www.farcountrypress.com.

Created, produced, and designed in the United States.
Printed in China.

13 12 11 10 09 08   1 2 3 4 5 6

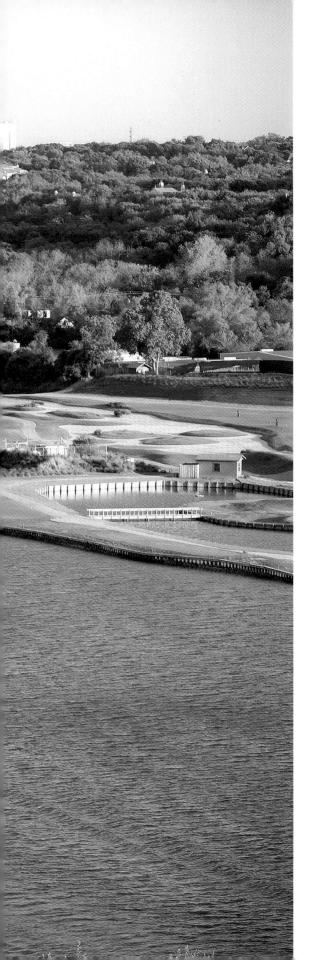

Above: Stephen F. Austin became "the Father of Texas" when he established the first Anglo-American colony in the Mexican province of Tejas in 1822 and later worked to create the Republic of Texas. This statue stands above his grave in the Texas State Cemetery.

Left: A boat speeds across seventy-five-foot-deep Lake Austin, created in 1939 by the construction of the Tom Miller Dam. With its largemouth bass, catfish, and sunfish, Lake Austin offers excellent angling opportunities. Note the skyline of downtown Austin in the background.

Right: Shortly before flowing into the Pedernales River thirty miles from Austin, Hamilton Creek falls fifty feet through limestone rock to form Hamilton Pool, centerpiece of Hamilton Pool Nature Preserve.

Below: Fed by an underground spring, Barton Springs Pool in Zilker Park maintains a brisk sixty-eight degrees year-round.

Facing page: Rising to nearly 516 feet, the Frost Bank Tower is covered in silver-blue glass; its crown is made up of more than an acre of white glass.

Below: As evening falls, the reflecting pool at the Palmer Events Center reflects Austin's modern skyline.

Above: Looking up into the Texas State Capitol dome, which rises 311 feet. The Renaissance Revival structure was inspired by fifteenth-century Italian architecture and was added to the National Register of Historic Places in 1970.

Right: Although it's made of Texas red granite, the 1888 state capitol gets a golden tint from the sun. With 392 rooms, it is the largest state capitol in the nation.

Above: The fountain at the Lyndon Baines Johnson Library and Museum, on the University of Texas campus, takes on a spectacular glow at night.

Left: Adorned with Christmas lights and luminaries, the Lady Bird Johnson Wildflower Center is dedicated to educating the public about native plants.

Above: A short drive from Austin are the clear waters of the San Marcos River, enjoyed by kayakers, canoeists, and divers.

Right: Aquarena Springs in San Marcos forms the headwaters of the San Marcos River, named by Spanish explorers who reached it on St. Mark's Day in 1689.

Left: The Long Center for the Performing Arts opened in 2008, its two theaters hosting a spectrum of live entertainment. The center is also home to the Austin Symphony, Austin Lyric Opera, and Ballet Austin.

Below: High on the University of Texas's Main Building, beneath the tower, the inscription reads, "Ye shall know the truth and the truth shall make you free."

Above: Movie-goers at the Alamo Drafthouse Cinema may order snacks, full meals, and libations during the films.

Right: At Driftwood, southwest of Austin, Driftwood Vineyards offers wine tastings and peaceful views of the Hill Country near Wimberley. Founded in 1998, the winery bottled its first wine in 2003.

Left: Rain cools runners in the Statesman Capitol 10,000, the state's largest annual 10K race.

Below: In 1986, as Texas celebrated 150 years of statehood, John Fisher created the Sesquicentennial Mural on the George Washington Carver Branch Library, portraying the search for black identity in America.

Above: A boater uses his crew shell to exercise on Lady Bird Lake.

Right: In the Blanco River Valley, a rare winter ice storm has eerily altered the landscape.

Above: Junction School in Lyndon B. Johnson National Historical Park, fifty miles west of Austin at Stonewall, is the one-room school the future president attended at age four, in 1912, for a few months until it was closed. His family then moved to Johnson City.

Left: President Johnson is buried in the family cemetery on the former LBJ Ranch, now the national historical park named for him.

Right: Following the death of Lady Bird Johnson in 2007, Town Lake was renamed Lady Bird Lake in honor of her efforts, along with many other leaders, to restore parkland on the shores of Austin's largest lake.

Below: Bluebonnets, the Texas state flower, and prickly poppies flourish in the Llano County countryside northwest of Austin.

Above and left: Couples dance to the unique rockabilly sounds of the Jesse Dayton Band at the Broken Spoke. Calling itself "the last of the true Texas dance halls," the Broken Spoke is where real country music has been featured since Bob Wills and the Texas Playboys helped invent Western swing.

Right: The Guadalupe River runs through the Texas Hill Country near Gruene.

Below: Blues guitar legend Stevie Ray Vaughn, a Dallas native, often performed his blues rock at various venues in Austin and is honored by a statue at Lady Bird Lake.

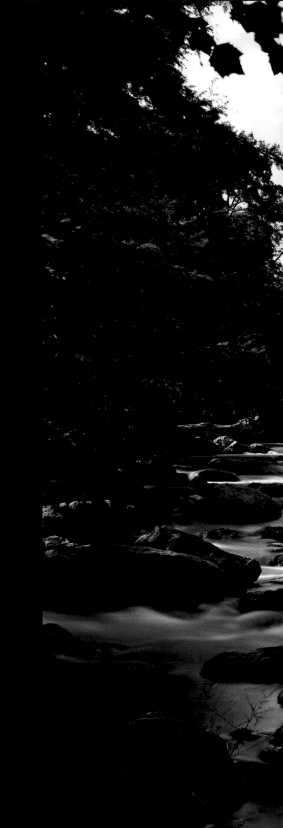

Above: The folks at family-owned Capitol Saddlery have been handmaking saddles, horse tack, boots, cowboy gear, belts, bags, and briefcases since 1930.

Left: The Grassy Meadow portion of Selah Bamberger Ranch Preserve is awash in golden hues at sunrise.

Right: Lyndon Baines Johnson said of his presidential library: "It is all here: the story of our time with the bark off. This library will show the facts, not just the joy and triumphs, but the sorrow and failures, too."

Below: Having served as the General Land Office beginning in the 1850s, today this historic building is the Capitol Visitor Center.

Left: The Pennybacker Bridge, named for a state highway engineer, went into service in late 1982. The longest steel-arch bridge in Texas, it carries the roadway over Lake Austin on a support that stretches from bank to bank.

Below: Barton Creek Greenbelt along the Colorado River treats Austin residents like this angler to easy outdoor access right in the city.

Above and facing page: Located on the former Circle Bar Ranch near Johnson City, Pedernales Falls State Park occupies more than 5,000 acres along the Pedernales River. These tranquil falls can swell to a massive torrent within minutes during Hill Country flash floods.

Above and right: Outside the Bob Bullock Texas State History Museum, a thirty-foot-tall bronze Lone Star greets visitors. Inside, three floors of interactive exhibits, an IMAX theater, and more tell the Lone Star State's story. One-time lieutenant governor Bob Bullock was a major supporter of building the museum, which opened in 2001.

Above: Greek and Roman sculptures on exhibit in the Michener Gallery, Blanton Museum of Art at the University of Texas, are among 17,000 works from Europe and the Americas.

Right: The Michener Gallery's Rapoport Atrium hosts museum-opening receptions and other gala events.

bove: The Texas State Cemetery is sometimes called "the Arlington of Texas." Plots are available for
ertain state government officials and those who have made significant contributions to Texas culture
* history.

acing page: A water-skier flies across the surface of Lake Austin beneath the Pennybacker Bridge

Facing page: Last light falls on a downtown office building.

Below: Viewers crowd Congress Avenue Bridge to watch the continent's largest urban bat colony head out for its nightly hunt. An estimated million-plus bats live under the bridge from March through October.
© MERLIN D. TUTTLE, BAT CONSERVATION INTERNATIONAL.

Above: When Texas was a nation, a French chargé d'affaires represented his country in the capital city. Today his residence, completed in 1841, is the French Legation Museum, managed by the Daughters of the Republic of Texas.

Left: In Wimberley, Blue Hole is a swimming spot on Cypress Creek, named for its surrounding cypress trees.

Above: The Enchanted Rock batholith attracts rock climbers to its challenging

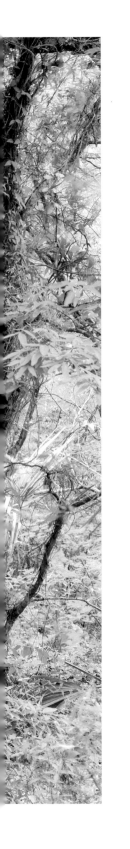

Above: Laguna Gloria was a private home on Lake Austin when completed in 1916, and later the home of the Austin Museum of Art. Today, the building houses the museum's art school and small exhibitions, with the main museum in a new downtown edifice.

Left: Laguna Gloria's twelve acres include sculptures, historic gardens, and rustic pathways.

Above: Every Saturday and Sunday, the Austin Steam Train Association makes a two-hour passenger run through the Hill Country, re-creating the days when steam locomotives tied the nation together.

Right: Open since 1878, Gruene Hall in the town of Gruene is the state's oldest continuously operating dance hall. Here, it's decorated for the holidays.

Left: St. Edward's University, founded in 1885, offers a Catholic liberal arts education to more than 5,000 students.

Below: With 206 parks, 12 preserves, and 26 greenbelts, Austin calls itself a "city within a park." Here, runners enjoy Lady Bird Lake's hike and bike trail.

Facing page: Milton Reimers Ranch Park, opened in 2005 and located west of Austin on the Pedernales River, offers serious rock climbing opportunities, bicycle trails, and plenty of peaceful views like this one.

Below: Lady Bird Lake is for nonmotorized boat use only, providing a placid spot in the center of Austin.

Left: Mammatus clouds grace the sky above the Hill Country following a violent thunderstorm.

Below: Dedicated in 1999 in the Texas State Cemetery, the Medal of Honor Monument honors Texans who have received the nation's highest military honor.

Above: Wild prickly poppies grow on dry, gravelly roadsides throughout the region. They have papery petals and a bright-yellow center.

Right: In the tiny Hill Country settlement of Twin Sisters, St. Mary's Catholic Church still hosts mass once a year, on All Saints Day.

Above: Outdoor dining over the waters of Lake Austin on a sunny summer day—what could be finer?

Facing page: Bald cypress trees line the Pedernales River on a Hill Country ranch.

Right: Hikers and picnickers climb Mount Bonnell's 700 feet of limestone
for this view of Lake Austin on the Colorado River.

Below: Young live oak trees, symbol of strength and also of the Deep South,
grow in the Hill Country.

Facing page: Architectural contrasts—old and new—on Congress Avenue.

Below: The University of Texas Longhorns take the field for a home game at Darrell K. Royal–Texas Memorial Stadium.

Above: Today, the Whole Foods Market chain has its headquarters and flagship store just blocks from where it began as a neighborhood shop in the 1980s.

Right: Bluebonnets, Indian blankets, and bitterweeds color the shore at Inks Lake State Park along the Colorado River.

Above: Littlefield Fountain on the University of Texas campus honors George and Alice Littlefield, a couple whose Victorian mansion was built in 1893 on what was then the edge of campus. Over the years they made many grand gifts to the school, including the still-standing home after Alice's death in 1935.

Left: In the Texas State Capitol, an illuminated Lone Star looks down on the Senate Chamber, which has been restored to its appearance of about 1910 and is furnished with the original walnut desks.

Right: The multi-use Palmer Events Center features a wraparound terrace and some of the best views of Austin and Lady Bird Lake.

Below: Barton Springs Pool in Zilker Park offers a three-acre swimming hole in which to escape the heat of summer.

Left: Comal County, southwest of Austin, is home to Fischer and its Fischer Hall dance spot, which has served the area since the 1890s.

Below: The Paramount Theatre in downtown Austin began as a vaudeville house in 1915 and continued as a grand movie palace through the eras of the flickers and the talkies. Today, it offers both live performances and classic films.

Above: Weighing up to eleven pounds, gray foxes live in the Hill Country around Austin, where they hunt by night, seeking birds, eggs, insects, fruits, and some nuts.

Right: Autumn strips the leaves from bald cypresses along Cypress Creek in Hays County.

Above: The Starlite Restaurant offers traditional Texas cuisine and other specialties in the city's Warehouse District.

Left: Backing up behind the 1941 Mansfield Dam on the Colorado River, Lake Travis extends for nearly sixty-four miles, offering all types of outdoor recreation and making a perfect Austin getaway.

Right: The Bickler Cupola in Zilker Botanical Garden serves as the backdrop for many a wedding portrait.

Below: In Zilker Botanical Garden, Isamu Taniguchi created a Japanese garden, which includes a traditional "Bridge to Walk over the Moon," where the full moon's image reflected in the water seems to follow walkers.

Left: Strings of lights form a giant Christmas tree when hung from one of Austin's historic "Moon Tower" streetlights in Zilker Park.

Below: Painkillaz rocks the crowd at Maggie Mae's, a fixture of Sixth Street, and Austin's music scene, for nearly three decades.

Right: Look closely for the peacock wandering through tranquil Mayfield Park and Preserve, which borders Lady Bird Lake.

Below: Built in what was countryside in 1855, the Neill-Cochran House displays Greek Revival architecture. The National Society of the Colonial Dames of America leads guided tours five days a week.

Left: Texas longhorn steers roam amid the bluebonnets at an Austin-area ranch.

Below: Since 1980, the George Washington Carver Museum and Cultural Center has been collecting, preserving, and interpreting materials from African-American history and culture.

Right: Once bordering the original University of Texas campus, the Littlefield House now sits among its many buildings. The historic home is a gracious setting for receptions and other functions.

Below: This Ornithomimus sculpture by John Maisano appears to stalk visitors in the Zilker Botanical Garden, where ancient dinosaur tracks have been found.

Above: The Texas State Archives building honors Lorenzo de Zavala, an author and signer of Texas's declaration of independence from Mexico, and longtime advocate of democracy in all of Mexico.

Left: Autumn arrives in the Hill Country, as seen from the Devils Backbone. Southwest of Austin, the steep, narrow ridge is topped with a curving highway that has become a popular scenic drive.

Above: The Dust Devils perform at the SXSW (South by Southwest) Festival, which includes music, film, and interactive technology. Its music performances add to Austin's reputation as "the live music capital of the world."

Right: Since the early 1980s, the Oasis restaurant above Lake Travis has billed itself "the sunset capital of Texas"—understandably so. After a 2005 lightning strike destroyed most of its decks, the owner rebuilt, with even more deck space.

Right: Granite boulders rest atop the dome of Enchanted Rock.

Below: The 1892 structure that was once the studio of portrait-sculptor Elisabet Ney is now a museum. With her husband, Dr. Edmund Montgomery, Ney helped establish Texas state universities and the Texas Fine Arts Association.

Above: Sunrise adds unusual color to the Frost Bank Tower's glass façade.

Facing page: At Lake Travis, soft sunset light closes the day.

Above: On the southwest side of downtown, the Warehouse District now houses upscale shops, trendy restaurants, and fine music venues.

Left: Indian blankets, bluebonnets, and other Texas wildflowers give this Mason County field a pointillist touch.

Right: After the first Texas State Capitol burned down in 1881, the new (and current) one was constructed from 1885 to 1888, with a dome seven feet higher than that of the United States Capitol.

Below: Nothing was too good for the Texas capitol, right down to the custom door hinges.

Above: Centerpiece of the Austin Museum of Art's Sunken Garden at Laguna Gloria, *The Poetess* looks skyward for inspiration. Sculptor Charles Umlauf taught for four decades in the University of Texas art department, and his work is found in public and private collections nationwide.

Left: At Lyndon B. Johnson National Historical Park, descendants of the president's registered Herefords are ranched in the environmentally conscious way he initiated here on the former LBJ Ranch.

Above: For seven blocks, Sixth Street forms an eclectic shopping and entertainment district popular with most everyone, regardless of their tastes in music or cuisine.

Right: The Continental Club, on South Congress Avenue, has been offering live music for more than a half century. In 1957 it opened as a supper club that hosted big bands, then switched to burlesque shows, and finally settled on rock performances.

Facing page: After this picture was made, the Greek Revival Texas Governor's Mansion was severely damaged in a June 2008 fire. Beginning with the fifth governor in 1856, the building had been the oldest continuously occupied governor's mansion east of the Mississippi River.

Below: Prickly poppies fill a Llano County horse pasture.

Above: For eight blocks where it passes the University of Texas, Guadalupe Street is known as "the drag," home to hip shops and eateries.

Right: Barton Creek flows into Lady Bird Lake below the Barton Creek foot and bicycle bridge.

ICE AGES

2 MILLION - 12 THOUSAND YEARS AGO

Above: Shhh…don't tell the children, but they're learning while playing with interactive exhibits in the Austin Children's Museum.

Left: The Texas Memorial Museum's Hall of Geology and Paleontology shows what this land's ancient denizens were like.

Above: Prickly pear cactus sports a toothy coat of ice after a Hill Country storm.

Facing page: Where water drips during summer, rare subfreezing weather builds icicles—
at Hamilton Pool in the nature preserve of the same name.

Following page: Downtown Austin awakens with the first light of day.